GLORIFYING GOD IN YOUR BODY

COMPACT EXPOSITORY PULPIT COMMENTARY SERIES

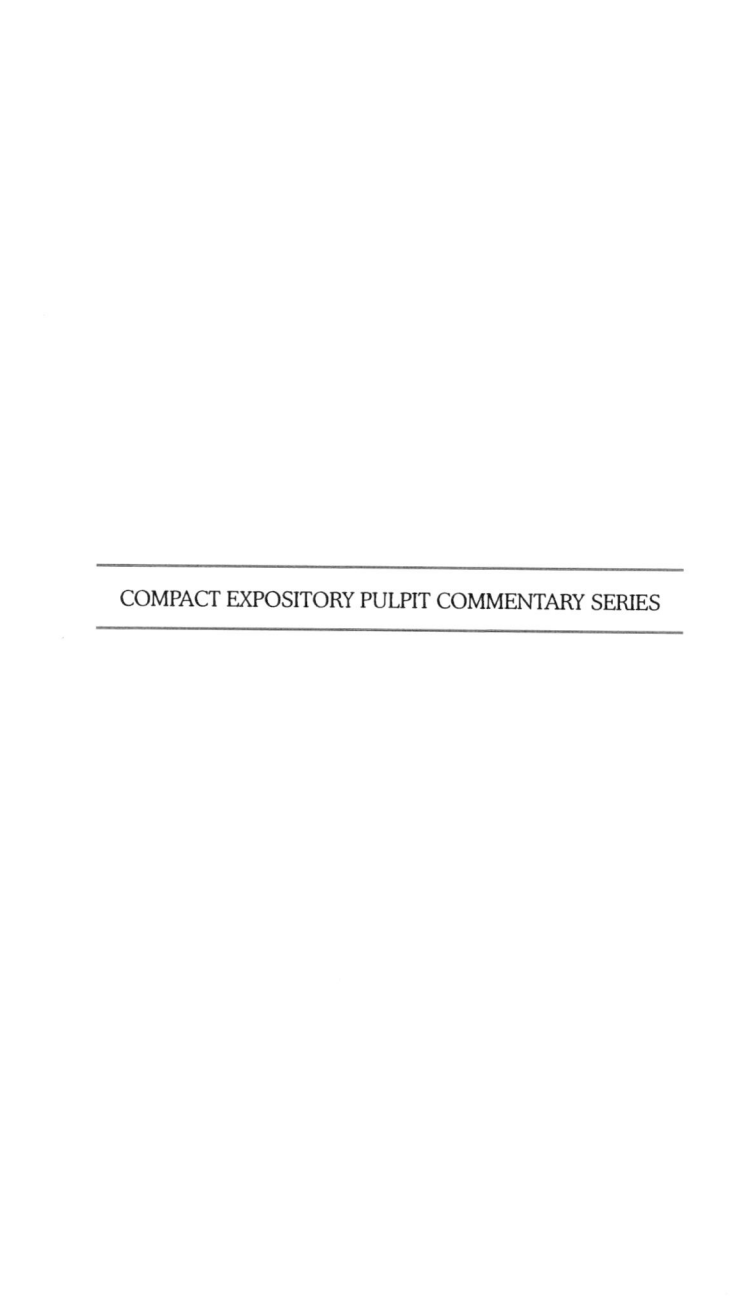

GLORIFYING GOD IN YOUR BODY

Seeing Ourselves from
God's Perspective

DAVID A. HARRELL

© 2020 David A. Harrell

ISBN 978-1-7359491-1-6

Great Writing Publications, 425 Roberts Road, Taylors, SC 29687 www.greatwriting.org

Shepherd's Fire 5245 Highway 41-A Joelton, TN 37080 www.shepherdsfire.com

All Scripture quotations, unless stated otherwise, are taken from the New American Standard Bible® (NASB), Copyright © 1960, 1962, 1963, 1968, 1971, 1972, 1973, 1975, 1977, 1995 by The Lockman Foundation. Used by permission. www.Lockman. org All rights reserved.

No part of this publication may be reproduced, or stored in a retrieval system, or transmitted, in any form or by any means, mechanical, electronic, photocopying, recording or otherwise, without the prior permission of the publishers.

Shepherd's Fire exists to proclaim the unsearchable riches of Christ through mass communications for the teaching ministry of Bible expositor David Harrell, with a special emphasis in encouraging and strengthening pastors and church leaders.

Table of Contents

Books in this Series 6

Introduction 7

Our Body from God's Perspective 18

The Sexual Revolution and Its Consequences 48

The Promise of Forgiveness, Deliverance, and Transformation 83

Endnotes 97

Books in this Series

Finding Grace in Sorrow: Enduring Trials with the Joy of the Holy Spirit

Finding Strength in Weakness: Drawing Upon the Existing Grace Within

Glorifying God in Your Body: Seeing Ourselves from God's Perspective

God, Evil, and Suffering: Understanding God's Role in Tragedies and Atrocities

God's Gracious Gift of Assurance: Rediscovering the Benefits of Justification by Faith

Our Sin and the Savior: Understanding the Need for Renewing and Sanctifying Grace

The Marvel of Being in Christ: Adoring God's Loving Provision of New Life in the Spirit

The Miracle of Spiritual Sight: Affirming the Transforming Doctrine of Regeneration

Introduction

Without fail, every person I have counseled who has struggled with some form of sexual immorality, gender confusion, or the male-female role relationships in marriage has had either a distorted or a non-existent understanding of how God views his or her body. Few people appreciate the astounding reality that "God created man in His own image, in the image of God He created him; male and female He created them" (Gen. 1:27). Even fewer enjoy the enormous blessings available to those who are committed to godly maleness and femaleness. With rare exceptions, most Christians never give much thought about being "made in the likeness of God" (James 3:9), yet the ramifications of being a man or woman created in His image are far reaching. Beck and Demarest summarize this well:

> The implications of human persons created in the image of God are immense for theology, psychology, ministry, and Christian living.

> Ramifications of the imago embrace issues of human dignity and value, personal and social ethics, relations between the sexes, the solidarity of the human family . . . and racial justice.[1]

It is axiomatic that as creatures we are obligated to submit to our Creator and not ourselves. To act independently according to our own standards—especially in the realm of morality—is high treason against the Most High and will certainly incur His wrath (Rom. 1:18). The apostle Paul described unbelievers as those who "exchanged the truth about God for a lie and worshiped and served the creature rather than the Creator" (v. 25). Because of man's depraved nature, rather than humbly bowing before God in joyful obedience, man is ruled by his lusts in defiance to God. "There is no fear of God before their eyes" (3:18).

There is perhaps no greater proof of man's innate hostility towards God's righteous standards than the staggering immorality of our postmodern culture—one that utterly rejects the authority of Scripture. Seldom does the authority of Scripture prevail in matters pertaining to sexuality, morality, and marriage. The final authority typically belongs to the wisdom of man, not the wisdom of God. Fewer and fewer evangelicals embrace the most fundamental of all truths that *as image bearers, we were created to give God glory*. Yet He has made this clear through the words of His prophet where He calls "sons" and "daughters" to worship Him—"everyone who is called by My name, and whom I have created for My glory, whom I have formed, even whom I have made" (Isa. 43:6–7). Indeed, "Whether, then, you eat or drink or whatever you do, do all to the glory of God" (1 Cor. 10:31). Obviously, this requires a clear understanding of our Creator's perspective of our bodies that He created and a heartfelt willingness to use them as He intended.

But sadly, this seems to be a topic unworthy of consideration, and certainly one that is being buried under an avalanche of cultural hatred toward biblical truth and all who submit to it. Notwithstanding the clarity of our calling to live for God's glory and the clarity of the standards of righteousness He has revealed in His Word, much of evangelicalism has caved in to the ungodly mob of the sexual, homosexual, and transgender revolution. Worse yet, these are major planks in the platform of the Democratic National Party (along with the killing of unwanted unborn infants). The moral free fall in our culture that began most visibly at the Woodstock music festival in 1969 has gained such momentum that there is more than sufficient evidence to say that America is now experiencing the wrath of divine abandonment in which God has lifted His restraining grace and now allows those who reject Him to experience the hideous consequences of their rebellion. Paul described it this way: "And just as they did not see fit to acknowledge God any longer, God gave them over to a depraved mind, to do those things which are not proper" (Rom. 1:28), a topic to be addressed more fully in chapter 2.

Moreover, it is appalling to witness the creative yet blasphemous ways the Bible is distorted among many professing Christians in an effort to embrace everything from homosexuality to transgenderism—as if they are morally acceptable in God's eyes. Worse yet, such blatantly unbiblical positions are boldly touted as being examples of Christian love when just the opposite is true. With the eternal souls of men and women at stake, there can be no greater act of hatred than to make people comfortable in their sin and thus doom them to God's righteous judgment; like the false prophets who "[strengthened] the hands of evildoers, so that no one has turned back from his wickedness. All of them have become to Me like Sodom, and her inhabitants like Gomorrah. . . . They are leading you into futility; they speak a vision of their own imagination, not from the mouth of the Lord" (Jer. 23:14, 16).

Having seen firsthand the dramatic conversion and radical transformation of those enslaved to many different forms of sexual perversions, I marvel at the transforming power of the gospel. Every Christian can rejoice in the words of the apostle Paul who, after warning fornicators, idolaters, adulterers, homosexuals, and sodomites that they would not enter the kingdom of God unless they embraced Christ in repentant faith (1 Cor. 6:9), went on to add these words of encouragement: "Such were some of you; but you were washed, but you were sanctified, but you were justified in the name of the Lord Jesus Christ and in the Spirit of our God" (1 Cor. 6:11).

But those who ignore God's standards of righteousness presume upon His merciful forbearance that is meant to lead them to repentance and forgiveness. As a result, they foolishly perceive any delay in divine retribution to be indifference, tolerance, or perhaps even agreement. What they fail to realize is God's compassionate delay in judgment also provides a season in which rebellious sinners can further harden their heart against the truths they resist and thus accumulate a greater store of wrath. This is a very dangerous reality that is too often ignored. Paul described it this way:

> Or do you think lightly of the riches of His kindness and tolerance and patience, not knowing that the kindness of God leads you to repentance? But because of your stubbornness and unrepentant heart you are storing up wrath for yourself in the day of wrath and revelation of the righteous judgment of God, who will render to each person according to his deeds.
> (Rom. 2:4–6)

We see examples of God's judgment upon the world for its gross immorality all through Scripture. In the days of Noah, demons inhabited human male bodies, took women to be their wives, procreated with them physically in an unnatural union (Gen. 6:1–4), and thus violated the God-ordained order of marriage and procreation (Gen. 22:24). We learn that "the Lord saw that the wickedness of man was great on the earth, and that every intent of the thoughts of his heart was only evil continually" (Gen. 6:5); and when "God looked on the earth, and behold, it was corrupt; for all flesh had corrupted their way upon the earth" (v. 11). As a result, God poured out his wrath on mankind through a global flood, saving only Noah and his family and two of every animal species (Gen. 7–8).

Similarly the forbidden perversion of homosexuality (Lev. 18:22, 29; 20:113; Rom. 1:26; 1 Cor. 6:9; 1 Tim. 1:10) ignited God's judgment upon Sodom and Gomorrah and the surrounding cities (Gen. 14:8; *cf.* Jude 7), when "the LORD rained on Sodom and Gomorrah brimstone and fire from the LORD out of heaven" (Gen. 19:24). Even Lot was "oppressed by the sensual conduct of unprincipled men" (2 Peter 2:7) in Sodom, "(for by what he saw and heard that righteous man, while living among them, felt his righteous soul tormented day after day by their lawless deeds)" (v. 8). The heart of every Christian should be likewise "tormented" by the rampant immorality that now defines our culture and is now being promoted in apostate churches that are "Christian" in name only.

But if we who are least holy are so grievously offended and distressed, what must be the reaction of Him who is most holy? The answer is found in Romans 1:19: "For the wrath of God is revealed from heaven against all ungodliness and unrighteousness of men who suppress the truth in unrighteousness." Indeed, "the wicked are reserved for the day of doom; they shall be brought out on the day of wrath" (Job 21:30); "For God will bring every work into judgment, including every secret thing, whether good or evil" (Eccl. 12:14). In fact,

Peter described the judgment of God that reduced Sodom and Gomorrah to ashes because of their sexual deviancy was "an example to those who would live ungodly lives thereafter" (2 Peter 2:6). Jude also cited Sodom and Gomorrah as examples of the kinds of sexual immorality and perversions of which the impostors he was confronting were accused saying,

> Just as Sodom and Gomorrah and the cities around them, since they in the same way as these indulged in gross immorality and went after strange flesh, are exhibited as an example in undergoing the punishment of eternal fire. (Jude 7)

Notwithstanding the justice we all deserve, God is merciful to those who are "humble and contrite of spirit and who tremble at [His] word" (Isa. 66:2). Though we "formerly lived in the lusts of our flesh, indulging the desires of the flesh and of the mind, and were by nature children of wrath" the Spirit "made us alive together with Christ" (Eph. 2:3, 5). At the moment of our new birth, we are made new creatures in Christ, setting into motion a process of sanctification that will ultimately conform every believer into the likeness of Christ. For "that which is born of the flesh is flesh, and what which is born of the Spirit is spirit" (John 3:6; John 1:13; 1 Peter 1:23). The Spirit plants within us new desires, loves, passions, inclinations, beliefs, and values (2 Cor. 5:17) so that we manifest the fruit of the Spirit: "love, joy, peace, patience, kindness, goodness, faithfulness, gentleness, self-control" (Gal. 5:22–23). By His power, we are able to "cleanse ourselves from all defilement of flesh and spirit, perfecting holiness in the fear of God" (2 Cor. 7:1).

As we examine the Scriptures together, we will quickly see that the wholesale celebration of sexual promiscuity and every imaginable form of degeneracy that is promoted in our culture is not at all new. In fact, the gross immorality we see today was every bit as bad in ancient times, if not worse. The saints in the early church encountered the same kinds of sexual perversions in their culture and in their church as we do today. However, sexual temptation, primarily through pornography, is far more accessible than in any other era of history, thanks to the Internet.

Moreover, we will see how the gospel changes everything! And when I say changes everything, I'm not merely referring to behaviors, but also *the desires that drive them*. Because every believer is united to Christ in His death and is forever hidden in

Him who has risen from the dead (Col. 3:3–4), we have the divine enablement to consciously slay the remaining sin that still cleaves to our unredeemed humanness.

> Therefore consider the members of your earthly body as dead to immorality, impurity, passion, evil desire, and greed, which amounts to idolatry. For it is because of these things that the wrath of God will come upon the sons of disobedience, and in them you also once walked, when you were living in them. (Col. 3:5–7)

Every true believer can rejoice knowing that the clear commands and instructions God has given us through the authors of His inspired Word not only help us understand how to navigate our depraved culture that is utterly saturated with sexual perversion and prurience, but also helps us know how to keep our hearts pure so we can live holy lives that are honoring to God and will therefore unleash His blessings and power upon us.

> For this is the will of God, your sanctification; that is, that you abstain from sexual immorality; that each of you know how to possess his

own vessel in sanctification and honor, not in lustful passion, like the Gentiles who do not know God.
(1 Thess. 4:3–5)

I trust your journey through these brief chapters will be edifying and encouraging as you seek to better understand what it is to truly *glorify God in your body by seeing yourself from God's perspective.*

1

Our Body from God's Perspective

Flee immorality. Every other sin that a man commits is outside the body, but the immoral man sins against his own body. Or do you not know that your body is a temple of the Holy Spirit who is in you, whom you have from God, and that you are not your own?
1 Corinthians 6:18–19

The people of first-century Corinth were exceedingly immoral. The most prominent edifice on the acropolis in Corinth was the Temple to Aphrodite, the Greek goddess of beauty, love, and procreation, where all manner of ritual prostitution and other vile forms of religious degeneracy were part of their "worship." Their debauchery was so pervasive and so vile that even the pagans blushed at it, so much so that they adopted the phrase, "to corinthianize" ("to behave like a Corinthian") to express the grossest kinds of sexual immorality and drunken decadence.

Temple excavations in Corinth have discovered thousands of terra-cotta votive offerings presented to Asklepios, the god of healing, and his daughter, Hygieia. Worshippers who sought healing would come to the temple to sleep and allow non-poisonous snakes to slither over them. The symbol of Asclepius was the snake. In fact, our modern medical emblem of a serpent entwined around a staff comes partially from this ancient cult. However, this demonic mythology can be traced back to ancient Egyptian, Sumerian, and Babylonian cultism where we see similar symbols. It should not escape our notice that Satan is often symbolized as a crafty serpent, even as he appeared to Eve in the Garden.

The Lord later describes him in Revelation 12:9 as "the serpent of old who is called the devil and Satan, who deceives the whole world." Ancient Gnosticism also used the emblem of a serpent as the embodiment of the wisdom transmitted by Sophia.

Clay molds of various body parts including various limbs, fingers, hands, feet, lips, noses, ears, breasts, male and female genitals, etc., were found in some of the chambers of these ancient Corinthian temples. Clay copies of human body parts were hung around the temple by worshippers in need of healing. But sadly, they did not know their diseased body parts were the result of the dreadful sexually transmitted disease of syphilis—a bacterial infection that can lie dormant for weeks, even decades, before becoming active again. Left untreated, it is fatal.

Even as God created and sustains a *physical order* to the universe that operates on fixed, inviolable laws of physics (like the law of gravity), He has also decreed a *moral order* to the universe. Though the consequences of violating His moral order are not always *immediate*, they are *inevitable* because God is holy and just, and therefore all sin must be punished (Rom. 1:18). That grisly scene of hanging body parts paints a graphic picture of sin and people's enslavement to it, for indeed, "there is a way that seems right to a man, but it is the way of death" (Prov. 14:12). People disobey God, thinking there's no consequence to their actions, yet all the while the wicked rebellion of their heart is metastasizing, corrupting both body and soul.

We see the physical consequences in diseases like HIV/AIDS and other forms of sexually transmitted diseases. A new strain of gonorrhea ("super gonorrhea") has now surfaced—a venereal disease that is reportedly resistant to all antibiotics normally used to treat the disease. This is truly terrifying since, according to the World Health Organization, gonorrhea infects approximately 87 million men and women every year.[2] It can even spread perinatally from mother to baby during childbirth.

Like idolaters today, the ancient pagans refused to worship the one true God. "Therefore God gave them over in the lusts of their hearts to impurity, that their bodies might be dishonored among them" (Rom. 1:24). No doubt that macabre scene of hanging body parts in the pagan temples influenced Paul's imagery of our bodies being a temple of the Holy Spirit (1 Cor. 6:19) and individual members of the body of Christ (1 Cor. 12:27).

Naturally, the profligacy of the culture greatly influenced the nascent church as it does in well-established churches today. The Corinthians were also heavily influenced by Plato's philosophical dualism that perceived matter as evil and spirit as good. The human body (and all matter) was considered inferior, bad, or evil. Socrates also believed in the superiority of the spiritual over the material and said: "The body is the tomb of the soul!" Because of this, the Gentile libertines—precursors of the Gnosticis—rejected all moral law and were essentially antinomians. They insisted that what a person chose to do with his or her body was meaningless. It was therefore not considered immoral to indulge the appetites of the body. Paul alluded to this by restating what was probably a popular proverb that celebrated the purely biological nature of sex when he said, "Food is for the stomach and the stomach is for food" (1 Cor. 6:13). And because indulgence in sensual pleasures is so appealing to the flesh, they appealed to Christian liberty to defend their lusts and justify their wickedness. Paul picked up on this in verse 12 (with what was probably another slogan) when he said, "All things are lawful for me, but all things are not helpful."

But Paul didn't simply say, "Stop doing these things!" Instead, he explained *why* and *how* to stop doing them, making his inspired words very instructive for those who struggle with various forms of moral turpitude in their life. Most fundamentally, *he wants us all to see our bodies from God's perspective—from a redeemed perspective—*by understanding four essential truths:

- Our body will be raised up through His power.
- Our body is a member of Christ.
- Our body is a temple of the Holy Spirit.
- Our body has been bought with a price.

Background: The Abuse of Christian Liberty

In dealing with the issue of Christian liberty (that they were abusing), Paul says: "All things are lawful for me" (the Greek verb *exestin* translated "are lawful" means, "it is allowed"). Paul is saying, "It is permissible for me to do anything" or "There is no law against anything that I want to do." Now obviously, "all things" do not include matters like those condemned in chapter 5 and 6:1–11 or other things God clearly forbids. But that is not what Paul is alluding to here. He's referring to non-moral issues—things not wrong *per se*, that is, behaviors that fall within the range of legitimate Christian liberty. So in that sense he agreed with their slogan. As believers, we are not bound to long lists of rules regulating what Christians may *eat, drink, and touch* (Col. 2:20–23). They have no bearing on our salvation. In these matters, believers have liberty of conscience: "You are not under law but under grace" (Rom 6:14); "But now we have been released from the Law, having died to that by which we were bound, so that we serve in newness of the Spirit and not in oldness of the letter" (Rom. 7:6).

This is cause for celebration. We are free from the condemnation of the law, no matter what we do. No sin will bring about a legal penalty. Christ has paid our sin debt in full. Indeed, "Who will bring a charge against God's elect? God is the one who justifies" (Rom. 8:33). For this reason Paul said, "It was for freedom that Christ set us free; therefore keep standing firm and do not be subject again to a yoke of slavery. For you were called to freedom, brethren; only do not turn your freedom into an opportunity for the flesh, but through love serve one another" (Gal. 5:1, 13). The problem with the Corinthians, however, was that they were turning their freedom into an opportunity for the flesh—and not through love serving one another, but serving their own fleshly appetites. The gospel they celebrated was not operating in their lives. They were more in love with *culture* than with *Christ*, ruled by their flesh, not by the Spirit.

So Paul picks up on their slogan and says, "All things are lawful for me, but not all things are profitable" (v. 12). It's as though he is saying, "You're not going to lose your salvation by committing sexual sin, but you will certainly forfeit blessing in your life." Sin never delivers what it promises—especially sexual sin that Paul is alluding to here. Indeed, "There is a way which seems right to a man, but its end is the way of death" (Prov. 14:12). This is a warning that should be repeatedly given to young adults in particular. The beautiful seductress may seem irresistible to a young man, "But in the end she is bitter as wormwood, sharp as a two-edged sword. Her feet go down to death, her steps take hold of Sheol" (Prov. 5:4–5).

There is certainly nothing more destructive in all of human existence than the effects of sexual immorality. Think of the tragedies stemming from sexually transmitted diseases, physical mutilation, unwanted pregnancies, great difficulties associated with single parenting and children raised without fathers, divorce, violence, abuse, suicide, and the list goes on. On hundreds of occasions I have counseled men and women whose marriage, family, and reputations have been ruined because of sexual sin. When someone calls me on the phone seeking help, I can always tell when the presenting problem is rooted in immorality. I've witnessed grown men and women sob so hard they cannot utter a word for extended periods of time, and when they do begin to speak, their words are almost unintelligible. Far too often I have had to deal with issues similar to David's sin with Bathsheba when he did "evil in the sight of the Lord" (2 Sam. 11:27), resulting in devastating long-term consequences (*cf.* 12:10–11, 14). John MacArthur summarized this danger when he stated,

Involvement in illicit sex leads to loss of health, loss of possessions, and loss of honor and respect. Every person who continues in such sins does not necessarily suffer all of those losses, but those are the types of loss that persistent sexual sin produces. The sex indulger will come to discover that he has lost his "years to the cruel one," that his "hard-earned goods" have gone "to the house of an alien," and that he will "groan" in his latter years and find his "flesh and [his] body are consumed" (Prov. 5:9–11). The "stolen water" of sexual relations outside of marriage "is sweet; and bread eaten in secret is pleasant"; but the dead are there" (Prov. 9:17–18). Sexual sin is a "no win" situation. It is never profitable and always harmful.[3]

While sexual enjoyment between a man and woman within the God-ordained parameters of the covenant of marriage is a wonderful gift from God (Gen. 2:18, 23–25), sexual activity outside the bond of marriage is strictly forbidden—including all fornication (Acts 15:29; 1 Cor. 6:9; Heb. 13:4), adultery (Ex. 20:14; Lev. 20:10; Matt. 19:18), bestiality (Ex. 22:19; Lev. 18:23; 20:15–16; Deut. 27:21), and homosexuality (Lev. 18:22; 20:13; Rom. 1:26–27).[4]

Sexual Slavery

Although most people will not admit it, sexual sin is enslaving. Paul stated this when he went on to say, "All things are lawful for me, but I will not be mastered by anything" (v. 12b). Paul was committed to personal holiness and testified how he had to "buffet [his] body and make it [his] slave, lest possibly, after [he had] preached to others, [he himself] should be disqualified" (1 Cor. 9:27). If we are living in the Spirit, we "are putting to death the deeds of the body" (Rom. 8:13). By the power of the indwelling Spirit we are able to *starve* our lusts rather than *feed* them, even as we would starve cancer cells in order to destroy them. So indeed, we are no longer slaves to sin; we are now free *not to sin*, "For sin shall not be master over you, for you are not under law but under grace" (Rom. 6:14). Charles Spurgeon elaborated on this warning:

> Sin is a domineering force. A man cannot sin up to a fixed point and then say to sin, "Hitherto shalt thou come, but no farther." It is an imperious power, and where it dwells it is hungry for the mastery. Just as our Lord, when he enters the soul, will never be content with a divided dominion, so is it with sin, it labors to bring our entire manhood under

subjection. Hence we are compelled to strive daily against this ambitious principle: according to the working of the Spirit of God in us we wrestle against sin that it may not have dominion over us. . . . Over the whole world sin exercises a dreadful tyranny. It would hold us in the same bondage were it not for one who is stronger than sin, who has undertaken to deliver us out of its hand, and will certainly perform the redeeming work.[5]

Using the Corinthian proverb that justified their immorality, Paul went on to say, "Food is for the stomach and the stomach is for food, but God will do away with both of them" (v. 13). He wanted them to understand that their stomach and food are temporal and that God is going to do away with all biological processes someday. Therefore their thinking was shortsighted and unspiritual. You might say they were thinking *horizontally*, not *vertically*. And then he added this profoundly insightful statement: "Yet the body is not for immorality, but for the Lord, and the Lord is for the body" (v. 13b). This is what most believers fail to accurately comprehend and wholeheartedly embrace: *Our body belongs to the Lord who created us, sustains us, redeems us, and will one day glorify us; and it is to be used for His purposes, not ours*. Sexual purity and the divine blessings that are the result of it cannot be attained unless a believer wholeheartedly embraces these truths.

Four Key Principles

It is most fascinating to consider Paul's inspired line of reasoning here. He only deals with sexual immorality as a secondary issue so he can focus on the primary issue of how Christians are to think in biblical terms about their body. And this brings us to the first key principle:

1. Our Body Will Be Raised Up through His Power.

Paul states, "Now God has not only raised the Lord, but will also raise us up through His power" (v. 14). Even as our Lord's soul was united with His body that was raised, our souls are also united with our body and will likewise be raised. This is an astounding promise that underscores the dignity of the body. But it was also a direct attack on the dualistic philosophical traditions advanced by the Greek philosophers Plato and Socrates that believed the human body—and in fact, all physical matter—is inferior to that which is spiritual.

Instead of the body being belittled, it is attributed

infinite worth. In contrast with the temporal nature of the stomach and of food that will both be destroyed (v. 13), God Himself will take the initiative and resurrect the body. Because we are united to Christ (Col. 1:27; *cf.* 3:3–4), though our body is subject to weakness and death, our body will be raised "imperishable . . . in glory . . . in power . . . a spiritual body" (1 Cor. 15:42–44). We will be given a body like Christ's glorified body, for He "will transform the body of our humble state into conformity with the body of His glory, by the exertion of the power that He has even to subject all things to Himself" (Phil. 3:21). For "we know that, when he shall appear, we shall be like him" (1 John 3:2).

Given the astounding reality that one day we will behold Him and be like Him in a glorified body that has been "raised through His power," we are struck by the profound importance of our body—a body that ultimately belongs to God, not us. The psalmist speaks to this most vividly when he says,

> For You formed my inward parts; You wove me in my mother's womb. I will give thanks to You, for I am fearfully and wonderfully made; Wonderful are Your works, and my soul knows it very well. My frame was not hidden from You, When I was made in secret, and skillfully

wrought in the depths of the earth; Your eyes have seen my unformed substance; and in Your book were all written the days that were ordained for me, when as yet there was not one of them. How precious also are Your thoughts to me, O God! How vast is the sum of them!
(Ps. 139:13–17)

Obviously, since our body belongs to the Lord, it should be treated with utmost care and respect and used for His glory. Because of His mercy, we are "to present [our] bodies a living and holy sacrifice acceptable to God, which is [our] spiritual service of worship" (Rom. 12:1). Similarly in 1 Thessalonians 4:3–5 Paul states, "For this is the will of God, your sanctification; that is, that you abstain from sexual immorality; that each of you know how to possess his own vessel in sanctification and honor, not in lustful passion, like the Gentiles who do not know God." We can rejoice knowing that the indwelling Spirit empowers us to maintain chastity outside of marriage and fidelity within the marriage covenant between one man and one woman. This power that is working in us is the same power that raised Christ from the dead (Eph. 1:18–19). We can all find great encouragement knowing,

If Christ is in you, though the body is dead because of sin, yet the spirit is alive because of righteousness. But if the Spirit of Him who raised Jesus from the dead dwells in you, He who raised Christ Jesus from the dead will also give life to your mortal bodies through His Spirit who dwells in you. So then, brethren, we are under obligation, not to the flesh, to live according to the flesh—for if you are living according to the flesh, you must die; but if by the Spirit you are putting to death the deeds of the body, you will live. For all who are being led by the Spirit of God, these are sons of God.
(Romans 8:10–14)

But Paul not only wanted the Corinthians to refrain from sexual immorality because their body belonged to the Lord and is so important to Him that it will be raised up through His power; he wanted them to also grasp a second profound reality:

2. *Our Body Is a Member of Christ.*

With the intention of jarring his readers, he asks, "Do you not know that your bodies are members of Christ" (v. 15)? The term "members" (*melē*) is the commonly used word for limbs and organs in the body (Rom. 6:13, 19). We are reminded in Romans 12:5, "We, who are many, are one body in Christ" (Rom 12:5), indeed, we are a part of the Lord's body, the church (Eph. 1:22, 23), a spiritual temple in which the Spirit of Christ dwells (2 Cor. 6:16).

One of the greatest metaphors in Scripture given to illustrate our union with Christ is the union of head and body: "Christ . . . is the head of the church, He Himself being the Savior of the body" (Eph. 5:23). In this context, Paul is urging husbands to love their wives who have become one flesh with them and must therefore be regarded as a single entity. Because of the intimacy of this union between the head and the body, the one who nourishes and cherishes his own body "loves himself. For no one ever hated his own flesh, but nourishes and cherishes it, just as Christ also does the church, because we are members of His body" (vv. 28–29). This example speaks of the intimate care Christ offers to His body, the church, in order to sanctify her (5:25–26)—a profound illustration of how the bodies of the redeemed are members of Christ's own body. What happens to the *head* happens to the *body*, and what happens to the *body* happens to the *head*.

With this in mind, we can better understand Paul's question to the Corinthians, "Shall I then take away the members of Christ and make them members of a prostitute? May it never be! Or do you not know that the one who joins himself to a prostitute is one body with her? For He says, 'The two shall become one flesh'" (v. 16). The physical union of sexual relations is only permissible in the bond of marriage where a man and a woman become "one flesh" (Gen. 2:24)—which speaks of a complete unity of parts making a whole; it implies sexual completeness where one man and one woman constitute a pair to reproduce. For a believer, sexual relations always involve the Lord because we are members of His body! Paul's point is obvious: *To join yourself to a prostitute (or some other person who is not your spouse) is to join Christ with that same person.*

Paul goes on to say, "But the one who joins himself to the Lord is one spirit with Him" (v. 17). When we are *born again*, Christ dwells in us in a wondrous mystical union so that *His Spirit and our spirit become one.* Jesus says, "That which is born of the flesh is flesh, and that which is born of the Spirit is spirit" (John 3:6); and Peter says, "We have become partakers of the divine nature" (2 Peter 1:4). It is therefore unthinkable that we would ever involve the infinitely holy body and Spirit of Christ in a physical union that He finds reprehensible; a sinful union that resulted in unimaginable suffering and pain when He bore our sins in His body on the cross!

The seventeenth-century English Puritan, Thomas Manton (1620–1677), described it this way:

> Where there is union and communion with Christ, there his Spirit is given to us, and they that have the Spirit of Christ will be like him; the Spirit worketh uniformly in head and members. . . . The bodies of the faithful are a part of his mystical body, and therefore must be used with reverence, and possessed in sanctification and honour; not given to a harlot, but reserved for Christ. He proveth the argument on both parts, that he that is joined to a harlot maketh himself one with a harlot, and he that is joined to Christ becometh one with Christ . . . . Do we dwell in Christ, and make Christ's mystical body a shelter and sanctuary for sinners, and this great mystery of union with Christ only a cover for a carnal heart and life? Surely every one that is in Christ hath greater obligations than others, being taken into such a nearness to God; and has greater helps, having received of his fullness, John 1:16. They have grace from him, as the branches have sap from the root.[6]

No wonder Paul says, "Flee immorality" (v. 1)—

an imperative that means *he is to run from it and not stop running*. No doubt Paul had in mind Joseph's example of fleeing from Potiphar's wife (Gen. 39:11, 12). Too often we find ourselves running toward it rather than fleeing from it. In 2 Timothy 2:22 he adds, "Now flee from youthful lusts and pursue righteousness, faith, love and peace, with those who call on the Lord from a pure heart." The exhortation extends to all believers. When it comes to matters of sexual immorality, he's saying in essence, "Don't dabble in it, think about it, or entertain it in your imagination. Station guards around your mind and shield your eyes." Solomon put it this way: "Watch over your heart with all diligence, for from it flow the springs of life" (Prov. 4:23).

We must learn to kill our lusts of the flesh still remaining in the body as a result of our depraved nature, "for if you are living according to the flesh, you must die; but if by the Spirit you are putting to death the deeds of the body, you will live" (Rom. 8:13b). When we kill something, we deprive it of its strength, its energy, and its power to exert itself. Sexual immorality is like a toxic poison that must be avoided at all costs. Whether it's seductive clothing, pornography, or sexually explicit movies, we must "[put] to death the deeds of the body" (v. 13), never feed them. We must also establish non-negotiable rules in how we interact with those of the opposite sex. We must avoid subtle flirting and flee from the sensual flattery of an adulterer (Prov. 7:5): "Do not let your heart turn aside to her ways, do not stray into her paths. For many are the victims she has cast down, and numerous are all her slain. Her house is the way to Sheol, descending to the chambers of death" (vv. 25–27).

Married men and women should never be alone with someone of the opposite sex—especially if they find them attractive. No private texts, off-line conversations, or subtle come-on gestures or remarks. Many naïve and immature believers walk on the very edge of the slippery slope of sexual sin rather than running in the opposite direction. God's wise warning through Solomon to avoid a seductive woman must not go unheeded: "Keep your way far from her and do not go near the door of her house" (Prov. 5:8). He goes on to warn:

> For the commandment is a lamp and the teaching is light; and reproofs for discipline are the way of life to keep you from the evil woman, from the smooth tongue of the adulteress. Do not desire her beauty in your heart, nor let her capture you with her eyelids. For on account of a harlot one is reduced to a loaf

of bread, and an adulteress hunts for the precious life. Can a man take fire in his bosom and his clothes not be burned? Or can a man walk on hot coals and his feet not be scorched? So is the one who goes in to his neighbor's wife; whoever touches her will not go unpunished. (Prov. 6:23–29)

Solomon's warnings help us better understand the dangers described in Paul's warnings to Timothy and, by extension, to every believer: "Flee immorality. Every other sin that a man commits is outside the body, but the immoral man sins against his own body" (v. 18). Unlike other sins, sexual sin is unique in that it arises from within the body as a powerful lust seeking gratification, but like all lusts, it can *never be satisfied*. Worse yet, it corrupts and wounds at the deepest level of our being! It produces untold misery, guilt, shame, anxiety, depression, divorce, violence, abortion, and disease.

But I'm not convinced this is only what Paul has in mind. I believe he's saying that unlike other sins that a man commits *outside his body*, sexual sin attacks our body by *uniting it to another person in a forbidden union*—an act that is a totally inconsistent with the truth about our body—that it belongs to Christ. We are united to Christ. So in that way, the immoral man or woman sins against his or her own body. For example, sexual sin commingles a man's life with a harlot and gives her what rightfully belongs to his own body that ultimately belongs to Christ. What a profound indignity to the body we possess by God's grace, a body eternally united to Him and inhabited by Him!

In the core of his or her being, every believer must be governed by gospel principles that automatically flow from the heart, inform the mind, and activate the will. We must all be able to say with heartfelt conviction,

> I know that God set His love upon me in eternity past; that He has created me, that He bore my sins in His body and thus purchased my redemption with His very blood; He inhabits me, and in Him I live and move and exist; my body is the limbs and organs of Christ; my body is not my own, it belongs to Him; it is the temple of the Holy Spirit and will be raised up through His power. Given all this, how can I possibly sin against my body through acts of sexual immorality? This goes against the very core of my new nature! It would be a sin that is not wrought from outside the body, but from *within itself*!

For this reason, the Christian experiences an even greater sense of guilt and shame than a non-believer when he or she commits sexual sins. All the more reason to heed Paul's warning and "flee immorality" (v. 18). Paul underscored this danger when he wrote,

> Do not let sin reign in your mortal body so that you obey its lusts, and do not go on presenting the members of your body to sin as instruments of unrighteousness; but present yourselves to God as those alive from the dead, and your members as instruments of righteousness to God. For just as you presented your members as slaves to impurity and to lawlessness, resulting in further lawlessness, so now present your members as slaves to righteousness, resulting in sanctification.
> (Rom. 6:13, 19)

Not only is our body going to be *raised up by His power* because it is a *member of Christ's body*, but our body is also a *temple of the Holy Spirit*, a third key principle that every believer should remember.

3. Our Body Is a Temple of the Holy Spirit

Using a form of irony to remind the Corinthian saints that their bodies are not their own, the apostle poses this question: "Or do you not know that your body is a temple of the Holy Spirit who is in you, whom you have from God, and that you are not your own?" (v. 19). This is a fascinating and most compelling line of reasoning.

Think about it: at salvation, we enter the kingdom of God where the Triune God Himself takes up residence in our hearts. Jesus said, "If anyone loves Me, he will keep My word; and My Father will love him, and We will come to him and make Our abode with him" (John 14:23). Indeed, "We are a temple of the living God" (2 Cor. 6:16), a spiritual temple in which the Spirit of Christ dwells (1 Cor. 3:16; Rom. 8:9). He sanctifies both our bodies and our souls, causing Paul to pray, "Now may the God of peace Himself sanctify you entirely; and may your spirit and soul and body be preserved complete, without blame at the coming of our Lord Jesus Christ" (1 Thess. 5:23).

Given these magnificent realities, the apostle forces the question: "Are you're going to bring a harlot or an adulteress or some other person into the sacred sanctuary of God to commit acts of sexual immorality?" Obviously, such an act would be a supreme act of blasphemy. Concerning this Thomas Manton writes:

> If you consider (the body) as the temple of the Holy Ghost, it is a dishonour to the body to make it a channel for lust to pass through. Shall we make a sty of a temple? Abuse that to so vile a purpose which the Holy Ghost hath chosen to dwell in, to plant it into Christ as a part of his mystical body, to use it as an instrument in God's service, and finally to raise it out of the grave, and conform it to Christ's glorious body? The dignity of the body well considered is a great preservative against lust.[7]

Whenever we find ourselves being "carried away and enticed by [our] own lusts" (James 1:14) to yield to some form of sexual temptation that we know in our conscience is dishonoring to God and will therefore cause us to forfeit blessing and initiate divine chastening, we must remember that our contemplated sin will not be committed alone or in secret. The Lover our soul who suffered and died for our sin will witness the offense in His sanctuary, our body; *because our body is a temple of the Holy Spirit*. H. B. Swete summarized it well when he said,

The general lesson is clear: You are God's consecrated shrine, through the Spirit's indwelling, and you are therefore relatively holy; beware lest your relation to the Holy Spirit be your ruin. . . . The body has been sanctified; let it fulfill its proper end, that of bringing glory to God whose temple it is.[8]

As believers, we have an obligation to honor God, to "make it as our ambition to be pleasing to God" (2 Cor. 5:9); "to present [our] bodies a living and holy sacrifice, acceptable to God, which is [our] spiritual service of worship" (Rom. 12:1). After all, our body will be raised up by His power because it is a member of Christ's body, a temple of the Holy Spirit. But there's a fourth great doctrinal truth that Paul asserts in his warnings to the Corinthians (and to all believers), namely, *our body has been bought with a price*.

4. Our Body Has Been Bought with a Price

Having exposed the blasphemy and danger of defiling God's dwelling place, Paul brings yet one final argument against sexual immorality: "For you have been bought with a price: therefore glorify God in your body" (v. 20). To treat with disregard what God has purchased by His very blood is a com-

43

mon reality of our fallen nature, especially when the seemingly irresistible power of inflamed sexual passions has been fanned into a roaring inferno through the habitual indulgence of illicit sexual desires and activities.

Paul's argument forced them to ask the question: "Have we forgotten that we are a debtor to God's grace?" Given the prevalence of profligacy among them, the answer was yes. With the same concern, Peter exhorts Christians in these words: "Conduct yourselves in fear during the time of your stay upon earth; knowing that you were not redeemed with perishable things like silver or gold from your futile way of life inherited from your forefathers, but with precious blood, as of a lamb unblemished and spotless, the blood of Christ" (1 Peter 1:18–19).

Treating with indifference the infinitely high cost of redemption is certainly to be expected among those who don't see themselves as all that sinful, or God as all that holy. Popular gospel invitations today where sinners are asked to "make a decision for Christ," or "accept Jesus as your personal Savior," or "ask Jesus to come into your heart" (terminology not found in Scripture) eliminate the need for heartfelt repentance like that of the tax collector who "was unwilling to lift up his eyes to heaven, but was beating his breast, saying, 'God, be merciful to me, the sinner!'" (Luke 18:13). If sinners fail to grasp how they have offended the holiness of God, they will have no real appreciation for the price He paid for their redemption. Worse yet, "by accepting Jesus into their heart" they will not only assume God is subject to their will in salvation, but they will also assume their belief in certain facts about Jesus settles all matters pertaining to salvation and obedience. Consequently, the need to submit to His lordship will be considered a non-essential option without consequence.

In his seminal work, *The Gospel According to Jesus*, John MacArthur addresses this issue, not only as it relates to the scandalous exhibitions of sexual degeneracy in the ranks of evangelicalism, but also the very definition of authentic faith.

> The gospel in vogue today holds forth a false hope to sinners. It promises them that they can have eternal life yet continue to live in rebellion against God . . . . It offers false security to people who revel in the sins of the flesh and spurn the way of holiness. By separating faith from faithfulness, it teaches that intellectual assent is a valid as wholehearted obedience to the truth. Thus the good news of Christ has

given way to the bad news of an insidious easy-believism that makes no moral demands on the lives of sinners.... This new gospel has spawned a generation of professing Christians whose behavior is indistinguishable from the rebellion of the unregenerate.... The church's witness to the world has been sacrificed on the altar of cheap grace. Shocking forms of open immorality have become commonplace among professing Christians. And why not? The promise of eternal life without surrender to divine authority feeds the wretchedness of the unregenerate heart. Enthusiastic converts to this new gospel believe their behavior has no relationship to their spiritual status—even if they continue wantonly in the grossest kinds of sin and expressions of human depravity.[9]

When something is considered to have little value, it will have little influence on our life. A $15 bottle of Extra Strength Tylenol used to cure an occasional ache will not have the same value as a $15,000 life-saving drug. Likewise, sexual immorality is an insult to God's gift of saving grace. Moreover, because He has purchased us with His blood, we belong to Him. To then commit acts of immorality in violation of His orders would be a sacrilege of the highest order. Instead, we need to heed the apostle's command: "You have been bought with a price: therefore glorify God in your body" (v. 20). Understanding these great truths adds even more weight to Paul's admonition:

> But immorality or any impurity or greed must not even be named among you, as is proper among saints; and there must be no filthiness and silly talk, or coarse jesting, which are not fitting, but rather giving of thanks. For this you know with certainty, that no immoral or impure person or covetous man, who is an idolater, has an inheritance in the kingdom of Christ and God.
> (Eph. 5:3–5)

May we all bow in humble obedience to these truths for our good and His glory!

2

The Sexual Revolution and Its Consequences

For even though they knew God, they did not honor Him as God or give thanks, but they became futile in their speculations, and their foolish heart was darkened. Professing to be wise, they became fools . . . . Therefore God gave them over in the lusts of their hearts to impurity, so that their bodies would be dishonored among them.
Romans 1:21–2, 24

The apostle Paul's words recorded in the inspired text of Romans 1:24–32 are the most sobering and terrifying section in his epistle. They should cause each of us to shiver with solemn reflection about ourselves, and those we know and love. Here we learn what happens *when God rejects man because man has rejected God*. Here we see the tragic consequences when God removes all restraint and lets a society indulge its every lust. When a culture reaches this stage of depravity, God allows it to gradually experience the terrible miseries of its sinful choices. This is best described as the *wrath of divine abandonment*—a terrifying fate that can lead to eternal abandonment for those who never repent, for "it is appointed for men to die once and after this comes judgment" (Heb. 9:27).

In order to explain why people stand guilty and condemned before God, Paul spent 67 verses (1:18–3:20) exposing the myth of man's perceived innate goodness, thereby justifying God's judgment upon sinners. And in chapter 1:23–32, he paints a vivid picture of what happens when someone "suppresses the truth in unrighteousness" (v. 18); when that person rejects God's revelation of Himself in creation and conscience (vv. 19–21) and chooses instead to worship himself or bows down to idols made with his own hands and honors the creature rather than the Creator (vv. 22–23). As stated earlier, *when man rejects God, God rejects man*.

To express this, three times Paul uses the phrase

"God gave them over" (vv. 24, 26, 28). This translates the Greek verb *paradidōmi*, a very strong verb meaning to "deliver up" used in the New Testament in a judicial sense to refer to one who is handed over to another for judgment (Matt. 5:25; 10:17, 19, 21; 18:34). In this context, God "delivers up" or "gives a man over" to the folly of his sin, causing him to experience the miserable consequences it will bring. Why? That he might finally come to a place of repentance, thus making God's abandonment a final act of mercy.

We must remember, God is never passive when evil is on the march. Although His judgment is always active, it is not always administered by an active outpouring of His wrath. Often, He will lift His restraint against the forces of evil and allow them to freely run their course of destruction. Describing Israel's rebellion, God said, "So I gave them over to the stubbornness of their heart, to walk in their devices" (Ps. 81:12).

Because sin is a metastasizing corruption, it will always take a person from bad to worse. Like cancer, it is never satisfied with a part; it always wants the whole. When it comes to sin—apart from the work of sanctifying grace—the spiral of one's life will always be *downward*, never *upward*. We witness this in our modern age where idolatry and gross immorality is gaining momentum as the world is being prepared for the ultimate deceptions of the Antichrist (2 Thess. 2:9–12) and the judgment to come (Rev. 20:11–15).

It is important to note, however, that grace will remain available to penitent sinners until their heart becomes so hardened that the Lord closes the door in their life—a time known only to God. So this is not eternal abandonment. Over and over again in Scripture, we see how the Lord is longsuffering, "not wishing for any to perish but for all to come to repentance" (2 Peter 3:9). But we must also recognize that the context here in Romans 1 is God's wrath revealed (v. 18), and if a man remains impenitent toward God, he will eventually cross a line known only to God from which he can never return. And when that occurs, *God will sentence him and abandon him for eternity.*

Here we discover three progressive stages of this abandonment—stages not necessarily found in every individual, but in the collective whole of a culture that magnifies its rebellion against God, primarily through gross immorality with each stage becoming progressively worse in its evil and in its consequences. First, God gives them over to *sordid immorality*, second, to *shameless homosexuality*, and finally, to *shocking depravity*.

Stage One: Sordid Immorality—a Violation of God's Moral Order

Paul describes this first stage of divine abandonment by saying, "Therefore God gave them over in the lusts of their hearts to impurity, that their bodies might be dishonored among them" (v. 24). This speaks of a *perversion of God's moral order that limits sexual activity to the union of one man and one woman in the God-ordained covenant of marriage* (Gen. 2:23–24; *cf.* Matt. 19:4–6; Eph. 5:31–32). Paul underscores this principle when he says, "But because of the temptation to sexual immorality, each man should have his own wife and each woman her own husband" (1 Cor. 7:2).

The Greek term *epithumia* (translated "lust") simply denotes the idea of longing or desiring a specific object. In biblical terms, a desire can be good or bad, depending upon the object desired. It is translated *lust* when the object desired is bad, and *desire* if the object has a neutral connotation (e.g., 1 Tim. 3:1). Here in Romans 1:24, Paul uses the term "lust" (*epithumeō*) to describe evil cravings, immoral desires, yearnings for that which God forbids.

Jesus uses the same term in Matthew 5:28 when He says, "You have heard that it was said, 'You shall not commit adultery'; but I say to you that everyone who looks at a woman with *lust* for her has already committed adultery with her in his heart" (emphasis mine). Lusting after a woman (or a man) proves a person "has already committed adultery" in his or her heart. Said differently, lust is a manifestation of an immoral heart rooted in our sinful nature. James warns, "Each one is tempted when he is carried away and enticed by his own lust" (James 1:14). Whenever the object of one's desire is for that which God forbids, the desire itself is sinful. Paul categorizes it as "the desire of the flesh . . . . For the flesh sets its desire against the Spirit" (Gal. 5:15). This also refutes the unbiblical notion that *same-sex attraction*—often referred to as *homosexual orientation*—is morally neutral unless it is acted upon since, because, as some will argue, "people cannot help how God created them." What they fail to understand is the attraction itself is sinful.

Jesus makes it clear that lust is rooted in "their hearts" (*kardia*), referring to the governing faculty of the person (Matt. 18:35; Rom. 6:17; 2 Cor. 5:12). The heart is the locus of man's thoughts, conscience, will, and emotion—that inner core and basic nature of who he really is as a person. It is the heart that "is more deceitful than all else and is desperately sick" (Jer. 17:9; *cf.* Prov. 4:23). For this reason Solomon said, "The hearts of the sons of men are full of evil, and insanity is in their hearts throughout their lives" (Eccl. 9:3). Jesus described it this way: "For out of the heart come evil thoughts, murders, adulteries, fornications, thefts, false witness, slanders. These are the things which defile the man" (Matt. 15:19–20). Paul reminded the saints in Ephesus about this very thing, saying, "We too all formerly lived in the lusts of our flesh, indulging the desires of the flesh and of the mind, and were by nature children of wrath, even as the rest" (Eph. 2:3).

Thus far in Romans 1, Paul has described the natural progression of the unregenerate human heart: it first suppresses the truth of God's character (vv. 18–20) resulting in a heart that becomes so increasingly darkened by sin (v. 21) that it becomes hideously arrogant (v. 22), idolatrous (v. 23), and immoral. As Christians, we are to "consider the members of [our] earthly body as dead to immorality, impurity, passion, evil desire which amounts to idolatry" (Col. 3:5). Idolatry not only describes those who reject or ignore God, but also those who entertain thoughts about God that are unworthy of Him. In both cases, these individuals create a god of their own liking and likeness. Historically, idol worship (which is Satan worship) breeds every imaginable form of sexual immorality and debauchery. Paul was very familiar with this in Corinth—a city notorious for these things. In fact, Corinth's temple had more than 1,000 priestesses who were nothing more than prostitutes. We also see this in the idolatry of the Roman Catholic Church where God and His ways have been grossly distorted and misrepresented; as a result, the scandalous sexual exploits of the Roman Catholic popes and priesthood are legendary.

Craving Impurity

So what we see thus far in this first stage of divine abandonment is that people who reject God are given over to their lusts because they have a heart craving for "impurity" (*akatharsia*), meaning "uncleanness" or "filth." This was a term used to describe the putrefaction of a corpse or the contents of a grave, which also became a synonym for sexual immorality. Paul used it in 2 Corinthians 12:21 where he expressed his concern for those "who had sinned in the past and not repented of the *impurity*, immorality and sensuality which they [had] practiced" (emphasis mine). The unregenerate are described as those who "walk in the futility of their mind, being darkened in their understanding, excluded from the life of God because of the ignorance that is in them, because of the hardness of their heart; and they, having become callous, *have given themselves over to sensuality for the practice of every kind of impuri-*

ty with greediness" (Eph. 4:19; emphasis mine).

So here we learn that when a man persistently rejects God, God will gradually give him over to a carnal craving for forbidden kinds of sexual immorality. Then notice the consequence: ". . . that their bodies might be dishonored among them." (v. 24b). When people indulge in these kinds of sins, their bodies are "dishonored" (*atimazō*), which means they are *treated shamefully and characterized by dishonor and a lack of respect*. The immediate context indicates that Paul had fertility cult ritual prostitution and habitual sexual contact with them in mind—central to their idolatrous practices. But their immoral worship would have also fueled the innate prurience of their depraved heart, spawning gross immorality at every level of their society as well.

But whether it's sexual immorality within the confines of pagan worship or the passionate lust for illicit gratification in general, in either case the body is dishonored. People cannot indulge in that kind of lifestyle and go unscathed. One look at a prostitute or one conversation with a "sex addict," or one testimony from a man or woman who has been involved in more sexual encounters than he or she can remember will affirm this.

Consequences of Moral Degradation

While the ultimate outpouring of this wrath upon the body is eschatological (i.e., it awaits the future and eternal wrath of God in hell), there are many ways in which the bodies of those who indulge in sordid immorality experience both physical and emotional dishonor in their bodies while yet alive on this earth. I have counseled young people who have contracted sexually transmitted diseases on spring break. Some strains of these diseases are becoming increasingly virulent and cannot be cured. There's also the guilt and physical suffering of abortions, the difficulties of single parenting, the trauma associated with relationships built upon lust rather than love, violence against women, and the self-hatred that comes from being used and using others often resulting in suicide. I've seen prostitutes in their thirties that look as if they are seventy years old. I've dealt with men so addicted to pornography that they find themselves in a vortex of lust from which they cannot free themselves, causing them to hate themselves and everyone around them. Mounce has rightly stated, "Moral degradation is a consequence of God's wrath, not the reason for it. Sin inevitably creates its own penalty.[10]

We need not look any further than the frightening statistics related to pornography:

1. Over 40 million Americans are regular visitors to porn sites. The average visit lasts 6 minutes and 29 seconds.
2. There are around 42 million porn websites, which totals around 370 million pages of porn.
3. The porn industry's annual revenue is more than the NFL, NBA, and MLB combined. It is also more than the combined revenues of ABC, CBS, and NBC.
4. 47% of families in the United States reported that pornography is a problem in their home.
5. Pornography use increases the marital infidelity rate by more than 300%.
6. Eleven is the average age that a child is first exposed to porn, and 94% of children will see porn by the age of 14.
7. 56% of American divorces involve one party having an "obsessive interest" in pornographic websites.
8. 70% of Christian youth pastors report that they have had at least one teen come to them for help in dealing with pornography in the past 12 months.
9. 68% of church-going men and over 50% of pastors view porn on a regular basis. Of young Christian adults 18–24 years old, 76% actively search for porn.

10. 59% of pastors said that married men seek their help for porn use.
11. 33% of women aged 25 and under search for porn at least once per month.
12. Only 13% of self-identified Christian women say they never watch porn—87% of Christian women have watched porn.
13. 55% of married men and 25% of married women say they watch porn at least once a month.
14. 57% of pastors say porn addiction is the most damaging issue in their congregation. And 69% say porn has adversely impacted the church.
15. Only 7% of pastors say their church has a program to help people struggling with pornography.[11]

Satan is introducing a new generation that is ruled by its sexual appetite—pornographers, pimps, prostitutes, rapists, pedophiles, homosexuals, transsexuals, transgender folks, adulterers, and fornicators—all "[given over] in the lusts of their hearts to impurity, that their bodies might be dishonored among them" (Rom. 1:24). As our Western culture continues to worship the human body, sexual immorality continues to dehumanize humanity at an alarming rate.

We must understand that sexual gratification outside the bounds of marriage between a man and a woman is actually a form of idolatry; and when people find their greatest joy in something other than God, they will habitually yield themselves to that object of worship until it defines their character (Ps. 115:8). What people fail to realize is that the idols they worship will ultimately testify against them (Rev. 21:8); indeed, "Those who cling to worthless idols turn away from God's love for them" (Jonah 2:8, NIV).

Our culture can be likened to prowling dogs and alley cats, utterly bereft of moral principles and dignity. Our women—including young girls—dress like trollops showing as much skin as possible (the tighter, the better), and our men mentally undress them as they walk by. Nothing causes us to blush anymore. The dirtier, the better; and no one seems to care—not even in many churches. I fear Hosea's warning is fitting for many within the ranks of evangelicalism today when he said, "Their deeds will not allow them to return to their God. For a spirit of harlotry is within them, and they do not know the Lord" (Hos. 5:4).

Given this, we should not be dismayed at the insanity of our political leaders, the riots in our streets, and the rapid demise of common decency and decorum in our culture. There is nothing sacred anymore, not even the sanctity of marriage between a man and a woman. Our country has become a nation of idolatrous sex worshippers and is now experiencing the wrath of divine abandonment! When a nation exchanges the truth of God for a lie, it will be *delivered over to that lie to become its slave and ultimately be destroyed by it.* God will abandon it to *sordid immorality—a violation of God's moral order* that will give rise to stage two: *shameless homosexuality—an inversion of God's created order.*

Stage Two: Shameless Homosexuality—an Inversion of God's Created Order

The next stage in the progression is described in verse 26: "For this reason God gave them over to degrading passions, for their women [lit. females] exchanged the natural function for that which is unnatural." The term "degrading" (*atimia*) speaks of that which is vile, disgraceful, or shameful. God abandons them to the vile affections of homosexuality.

Once again, in context, this is what happens when individuals exchange the truth of who God is for a lie. *Righteousness* will then be exchanged for that which is *unrighteous*, and what is *pure* will be exchanged for that which is *unclean*. Paul's use of "the natural" (*phusikos*) refers to that which is produced by nature, inborn, governed by the instincts of nature, and the term "function" (*chresis*) simply means "use"—the sexual use of a woman, referring to the normal, natural intimacy of sexual intercourse. That is exchanged "for that which is unnatural" (against nature, contrary to instincts that govern our behavior).

Obviously this is speaking of homosexual behavior among women. Unlike "sordid immorality" (a perversion of God's intention for sexual relations), homosexuality is an inversion of not only God's intentions for sexual relations, but it also defies man's nature that instinctively governs his behaviors. It is interesting that Paul mentions female homosexuality first, and male homosexuality second. Since females in a society are usually more reluctant than men to fall prey to sordid immorality—especially shameless homosexuality—perhaps by mentioning them first Paul is describing a culture where this form of idolatry is so rampant that all moral virtue has disappeared. That is certainly true in our Western culture.

The Inner Inferno of Homosexual Lust

He then goes on to add, "And in the same way also the men abandoned the natural function of the woman and burned in their desire toward one another, men with men committing indecent acts . . ." (v. 27). The term "burned" (*ekkaio*) means "to set on fire" or "to inflame." Because it is in the passive voice, he's saying, "They are set on fire in their desire," (they become inflamed or consumed with an unnatural craving to become sexually involved with another man). I have counseled a number of homosexual men who have described this to me. With deep frustration, one man described it as "an urge so powerful that I would have to kill myself to stop it." It is not at all uncommon for homosexual men to have over 100 partners per year (females average only one or two).

For those of us not enslaved by this sin, it is impossible to conceive of anything so life dominating. Genesis 19 provides an example of this in the account of the two angels that came to visit Lot in the city of Sodom. On seeing the strangers, "the men of the city, the men of Sodom, surrounded the house, both young and old, all the people from every quarter; and they called to Lot and said to him,

"Where are the men who came to you tonight? Bring them out to us that we may have relations with them. . . ." They pressed hard against Lot and came near to break the door. But the men reached out their hands and brought Lot into the house with them, and shut the door. And they struck the men who were at the doorway of the house with blindness, both small and great, so that they wearied themselves trying to find the doorway. (Gen. 19:5, 9–11)

Amazing! Their lust was so strong that, despite being supernaturally blinded, they still exhausted themselves to find the doorway to break in and have their way with the strangers. The text goes on to say that this sin was so great in Sodom and Gomorrah that God rained down fire and brimstone out of heaven upon them and utterly destroyed them. Unlike any other place in the world, deposits of sulfur (brimstone) capsules with a purity of 98 percent can still be found in layers of ash in this region. From Genesis 19 onward, the word "sodomy" is used to describe homosexuality.

Paul went on to describe this perversion in Romans 1:27 saying, "Men abandoned the natural function of the woman and burned in their desire toward one another, men with men committing indecent acts" (*aschemosune*: "that which is unseemly" or "shameful"; "males with males perpetrating shamelessness" [KJV]). How sad that they want to be called "gay" when they are anything but gay; they are filled with shame, guilt, frustration, helplessness, hopelessness, and rage. Yet they are constantly promoting "gay pride." This is reminiscent of the homosexual rebellion that contributed to the societal collapse of ancient Judah and triggered God's judgment upon them:

> For Jerusalem has stumbled and Judah has fallen, because their speech and their actions are against the Lord, to rebel against His glorious presence. The expression of their faces bears witness against them, and they display their sin like Sodom; they do not even conceal it. Woe to them! For they have brought evil on themselves. (Isa. 3:8–9)

God's Perspective and Prohibitions

Of course God's Word on the matter is meaningless to those who have rejected Him; but He has made it clear what He thinks of this as indicated in some of the passages of Scripture cited as follows:

- Leviticus 18:22: "You shall not lie with a male as one lies with a female; it is an abomination." God goes on to denounce bestiality that will inevitably be a part of an idolatrous culture that embraces homosexuality: "Also you shall not have intercourse with any animal to be defiled with it, nor shall any woman stand before an animal to mate with it; it is a perversion" (v. 23).
- Leviticus 20:13: "If there is a man who lies with a male as those who lie with a woman, both of them have committed a detestable act; they shall surely be put to death."
- Deuteronomy 23:17: "None of the daughters of Israel shall be a cult prostitute, nor shall any of the sons of Israel be a cult prostitute." In verse 18 God calls a male prostitute a "dog."
- In Judges 19:22–24, sodomites are called "worthless fellows" that commit "wickedness"; "an act of folly against a man."
- 1 Kings 14:24: "And there were also male cult prostitutes in the land. They did according to all the abominations of the nations, which the LORD dispossessed before the sons of Israel."
- 1 Corinthians 6:9: "Or do you not know that the unrighteous shall not inherit the kingdom of God? Do not be deceived; neither

fornicators, nor idolaters, nor adulterers, nor effeminate [the passive partner, transvestites, transsexuals], nor homosexuals [the active partner], nor thieves, not the covetous, nor drunkards, nor revilers, nor swindlers shall inherit the kingdom of God. And such were some of you; but you were washed but you were sanctified, but you were justified in the name of the Lord Jesus Christ, and in the Spirit of our God."

- In Ephesians 4:17 Paul speaks of the unsaved who walk "in the futility of their mind, being darkened in their understanding, excluded from the life of God, because of the ignorance that is in them, because of the hardness of their heart; and they, having become callous, have given themselves over to sensuality, for the practice of every kind of impurity with greediness." Then he adds in 5:11–12: "Do not participate in the unfruitful deeds of darkness, but instead even expose them; for it is disgraceful even to speak of the things which are done by them in secret."
- 1 Timothy 1:9: "[The] law is not made for a righteous person, but for those who are lawless and rebellious, for the ungodly and sinners, for the unholy and profane, for those who kill their

fathers or mothers, for murderers and immoral men and homosexuals and kidnappers and liars and perjurers, and whatever else is contrary to sound teaching.

Chilling Examples of Homosexual Conduct and Consequences

Having counseled homosexual men, and having worked closely with doctors and nurses who have attended them in the emergency rooms in local hospitals, I know far more than I wish I knew about the bizarre sexual practices in that community—sexual activities so vile that they can only be described as demonic. And sadly, but not surprisingly, their unsanitary activities in disease-ridden places not only transmit bacteria, parasites, and facilitate the spread of hepatitis B, HIV, syphilis, and numerous other blood-borne diseases, but they also tear rectal tissues.[12] But none of this should surprise us. Even Josephus, *Antiquities.* 1.194, stated that they "abused themselves with Sodomitical practices."[13]

Even as God has determined fixed, inviolable *laws of physics* to maintain the order of His physical order, so too He has determined fixed, inviolable *laws of morality* to maintain His moral order. The self-avenging nature of sexual perversion is evidence of what happens when a person violates God's law of morality, as in this case, "men with men committing indecent [shameful] acts and receiving in their own persons the due penalty of their error" (Rom. 1:27). Can there be a more tragic example of this than AIDS? The apostle's stern warning is deafening in this regard:

> Do not be deceived, God is not mocked; for whatever a man sows, this he will also reap. For the one who sows to his own flesh will from the flesh reap corruption, but the one who sows to the Spirit will from the Spirit reap eternal life.
> (Gal. 6:7–8)

In their excellent book, *Transforming Homosexuality: What the Bible Says About Sexual Orientation and Change*, Denny Burk and Heath Lambert offer additional insight into the many physical ways in which, under the moral management of God, gross immorality triggers its own "due penalty" (Rom. 1:27):

> Homosexuality is dangerous. *The Journal of the American Medical Association* reports that male homosexuals experience a 4,000 percent higher risk of anal cancer than the rest of the pop-

ulation. Male homosexuals with a long-term partner live, on average, thirty years shorter than heterosexual men. These and other factors are why homosexual men are at such high risk for emotional and spiritual problems.[14]

They went on to say that this was the conclusion of J. Michael Bailey concerning several studies on homosexuality:

> These studies contain arguably the best published data on the association between homosexuality and psychopathology, and both converge on the same unhappy conclusion: homosexual people are at substantially higher risk for some forms of emotional problems, including suicidality, major depression, and anxiety disorder, [and] conduct disorder.[15]

It is well documented by forensic experts who have examined thousands of autopsies that homosexual violence committed against another homosexual is among the most brutal of homicides. New York forensic expert Dr. Milton Helpern made this observation:

> When we see . . . brutal, multiple wound cas-

es in a single victim . . . we just automatically assume that we're dealing with a homosexual victim and a homosexual attacker. . . . I don't know why it is so, but it seems that the violent explosions of jealousy among homosexuals far exceed those of the jealousy of man for a woman, or a woman for a man. The pent-up charges and energy of the homosexual relationship simply cannot be contained. When the explosive point is reached, the result is brutally violent. . . . But this is the "normal" pattern of these homosexual attacks, the multiple stabbings, the multiple senseless beatings that obviously must continue long after the victim dies.[16]

According to the Family Research Institute:

The median age of death for homosexuals, however, was virtually the same nationwide—and, overall, about 2% survived to old age. If AIDS was the listed cause of death, the median age was 39. For the 829 gays who were listed as dying of something other than AIDS, the median age of death was 42 and 9% died old. The 163 lesbians had a median age of death of 44 and 20% died old.

Even when AIDS was apparently not involved, homosexuals frequently met an early demise. Three percent of gays died violently. They were 116 times more apt to be murdered (compared to national murder rates), much more apt to commit suicide, and had high traffic-accident death-rates. Heart attacks, cancer, and liver failure were exceptionally common. 18% of lesbians died of murder, suicide, or accidents—a rate 456 times higher than that of white females aged 25–44. Age distributions of samples of homosexuals in the scientific literature from 1858 to 1997 suggest a similarly shortened lifespan.

Follow-up studies of homosexual longevity have confirmed these general results. Comparison of gay obituaries who died of AIDS to official U.S. HIV/AIDS Surveillance data demonstrated very close agreement between the estimated median ages of death, as well as the 25th and 75th percentiles of the age-at-death distribution. Another study looked at multiple lines of evidence—including more recent U.S. obituaries and patterns of homosexual partnerships in Scandinavia—again finding that homosexual behavior was associated with a shortening of life of probably two decades.[17]

It is obvious to any unbiased observer that the inevitable temporal penalty of homosexuality is the consequences of the perversion itself—"men with men committing indecent acts and receiving in their own persons the due penalty of their error" (Rom. 1:27). However, unless they come to Christ in repentant faith and experience the transforming power of regeneration, the eternal consequences will be infinitely worse. The Bible is emphatic: "Just as Sodom and Gomorrah and the cities around them . . . indulged in gross immorality and went after strange flesh, are . . . undergoing the punishment of eternal fire" (Jude 7; *cf.* Rev. 21:8).

Once again, when man rejects God, God rejects man, and gives him over to *sordid immorality, shameless homosexuality*, which leads to the final stage of *shocking depravity*.

Stage Three: Shocking Depravity—a Disposition of Godless Corruption

The correlation in verses 24 and 26 between man's arrogant rejection of God and God's righteous rejection of man is stated again in Romans 1:28: "And just as they did not see fit to acknowledge God any longer, God gave them over to a depraved mind, to do those things which are not proper." The "depraved mind" shakes its fist in God's face and says, "Depart from us! We do not even desire the knowledge of Your ways. Who is the Almighty, that we should serve Him, and what would we gain if we entreat Him?" (Job 21:14–15).

Paul's use of the term "depraved" is most telling; it explains the utter irrationality and insanity that is now so pervasive in American culture. The Greek term *adokimos* translated "depraved" means "unapproved," "worthless," "useless." It was originally used to describe worthless metals rejected by refiners due to their impurity. In context, the phrase highlights a frightening reality: when man ignores all the evidence of nature and conscience and refuses to "approve" of God, he will be given over to an "unapproved" mind that is utterly worthless—*a disposition of godless corruption*. This is similarly stated in Titus 1:15–16: "To those who are defiled and unbelieving, nothing is pure, but both their mind and their conscience are defiled. They profess to know God, but by their deeds they deny Him, being detestable and disobedient and worthless for any good deed." Our culture's obsession with transgenderism is a prime example of a depraved mind.

Rather than rejoicing in God's goodness in creating a child in His image as male or female, an increasing number of parents embrace "Gender-Creative" parenting where a child is allowed to discover his or her own gender identity. According to Healthline.com, there are now sixty-four terms that describe gender identity and expression.[18] And what is even more shocking is the culture's acceptance of this kind of insanity. Dr. Michael A. Milton writes:

> Humankind's potential for self-destruction through the lusts of the flesh appears to be limitless. While there is nothing new in the sensual sins and wanton debauchery that we witness in our culture, technology has undoubtedly advanced its influence. And one such sin is being promoted in an apparently fanatical fashion: *transgenderism.*
>
> The subject of transgenderism, includes, specifically, *"Trans-sexuality, cross-dressing,"* and seeking *"gender identity development,"* i.e., *physical identity* through radical surgeries, and hormone treatment; and, more broadly, "gender atypicality" that includes "myriad subcultural expressions of self-selecting gender," and "intersectionality" with other "interdependence" movements, i.e., feminism, homosexuality. The idea of transgenderism has its roots in the primordial rebellion of hu-

mankind to the creation order of God.

Ancient pagan rituals would have included some aspects of transgender practice. More currently, social anarchists such as the otherwise brilliant French social critic, Michael Foucault, argued that Christianity, in particular, has leveraged its cultural "powers" (a recurring them with Foucault) to repress human sexual expression. Foucault taught that gender is a social construct, not a biological fact. The absurdity of such thinking was largely unchallenged in the 1960s and 70s when Foucault and others were teaching such dogma in prestigious universities in Canada, France, and the United States.

Perhaps, we felt that it was too ludicrous to engage. Recently, in 2019, when a former United States Vice-President was asked how many genders there were, he responded, "At least three." Such a frighteningly fallacious response by a person of influence constitutes an unmitigated endorsement of Foucault's radical deconstruction of reality. For someone to affirm, with a straight face, in serious dialogue, "There are at least three genders" is an Orwellian case study in "doublethink," "newspeak," and the "thought police" writ large.

To speak seriously about a gender other than male and female is surely the untenable subordinating to the inconceivable.[19]

The shocking depravity of "a depraved mind, to do those things which are not proper" includes a vast array of vices beyond the illustration of transgenderism. Paul goes on to give a representative sample in verses 29–31 describing the wickedness that characterizes a people given to idolatry and the concomitant immorality associated with it. He describes them as "being filled with" (v. 29), meaning they are wholly given over to the following:

- "all unrighteousness" (*adikia*): those whose heart and lifestyle consistently violate God's moral standard of righteousness found in His law (*cf.* Rom. 3:10–18).
- "wickedness" (*ponēria*): a synonym for unrighteousness describing those who enjoy perverting virtue and moral principles to do evil (*cf.* Jer. 4:22: 1 Cor. 6:9–10; Gal. 5:19–21; Col. 3:5).
- "greed" (*pleonexia*): those with an insatiable appetite for more and more possessions, never content or satisfied, bent on gaining what they desire no matter how it is achieved (*cf.* Mark 7:22; Eph. 6:12).

- "evil" (*kakia*): those filled with malice, cruelty, and a desire to injure others, unashamed to break the law (*cf.* Gen. 6:5; Isa. 5:20; 13:11; Gal. 1:4).
- "full of envy" (*phthonos*): those who are aroused to anger toward the success or possessions of another and begrudge them for having such (*cf.* Titus 3:3; James 3:16).
- "murder" (*phonos*): the unlawful killing of one human being by another; all the previous vices lead to this, especially envy (*cf.* Ex. 20:13; 1 Tim. 1:9).
- "strife" (*eris*): those who are habitually involved in bitter conflict, contentious debate, violent dissension (*cf.* Prov. 10:12; 13:10; 16:28; James 4:1).
- "deceit" (*dolos*): those who are cunningly dishonest, skilled in treachery, disingenuous, duplicitous, and crafty in lying (*cf.* Jer. 17:9; Rom. 3:13; 2 Tim. 3:13).
- "malice" (*kakoētheia*): those with a spiteful, cruel, depraved character, who are malicious and wily in harming other people (*cf.* 1 Cor. 5:8; Eph. 4:31; Titus 3:3).
- "they are gossips" (*psithyristēs*): those who whisper; secret slanderers who vilify others and spreads rumor to harm them (*cf.*

Prov. 16:28; 2 Cor. 12:20).

- "slanderers" (*katalalos*): those who speak evil of others in order to destroy their reputation (*cf.* Exod. 20:16; Lev. 19:16; Prov. 6:19).
- "haters of God" (*theostygēs*): those with excessive contempt for God (*cf.* Num. 10:35; Deut. 7:10; Rom. 8:7–8; James 4:4).
- "insolent" (*hubristēs*): those who are brazenly insulting, outrageously disrespectful and offensive; a "violent aggressor" (*cf.* 1 Tim 1:13).
- "arrogant" (*hyperēphanos*): those who are characterized by feelings of unwarranted importance, who consider themselves superior to others and despise those considered beneath them, treating them with contempt (*cf.* Ps. 94:3–7; Prov. 8:13; Isa. 13:11).
- "boastful" (*alazōn*): those who are a self-absorbed; a self-exalting braggart; an empty pretender proud without cause; one who is a legend in his or her own mind (*cf.* Isa. 14:13–16; Ps. 10:3; Prov. 25:14).
- "inventors of evil" (*epheuretēs kakos*): those who delight in devising novel forms of evil to destroy others and derive pleasure in finding new and creative ways to mock God (*cf.* Ps. 106:34–39; Prov. 24:8–9; Eccl. 7:29).
- "disobedient to parents" (*apeithēs goneus*): those

who refuse to submit to the parental authority God has placed over them (*cf.* Ex. 20:12; 21:15, 17; Prov. 20:20; Matt. 15:4).
- "without understanding" (*asynetos*): those who are senseless, stupid, foolish, undiscerning (*cf.* Prov. 18:2; Jer. 4:22; Rom. 3:11; 1 Cor. 2:14).
- "untrustworthy" (*asynthetos*): covenant breakers, those who disregard contracts and marital vows, and whose word means nothing (*cf.* Ps. 78:57; 119:158; Matt. 5:37).
- "unloving" (*astorgos*): those who are heartless toward those they should love, especially bereft of the natural affection toward children and family members (*cf.* Lev. 18:21; Ps. 106:36–38).
- "unmerciful" (*aneleēmōn*): those who are cruel, ruthless, merciless, heartless, and unsympathetic (*cf.* Matt. 18:32–34; James 2:13).

Examples of these crimes abound in our culture. Indeed, people are "filled with" them (v. 29). But Paul states the very pinnacle of perversity in verse 32: "and, although they know the ordinance of God, that those who practice such things are worthy of death," since God has revealed it to them in nature (1:21) and conscience (2:14, 15), "they not only do the same, but also give hearty approval to those who practice them." This is *shocking depravity*! Although their conscience is animated by the horrific fear of divine judgment, their heart has been so hardened by the deceitfulness of sin (Heb. 3:13) that they not only continue to "practice these things" but they encourage others to do the same. Indeed, today's society glamorizes the most deviant forms of sexual immorality. It elects officials to legalize, promote, and protect all manner of perversions. It worships artists and actors and authors and comedians who will advance the causes of the wicked and perverse. What should be considered shameful is exalted under a rainbow banner of "Pride!"

This is reminiscent of the defiant debauchery of ancient Judah that inflamed God's wrath against them and unleashed His judgment upon them. Using bitter words in Isaiah 5:18, God spoke through His prophet saying: "Woe to those who drag iniquity with the cords of falsehood, and sin as if with cart ropes; who say, 'Let Him make speed, let Him hasten His work, that we may see it; and let the purpose of the Holy One of Israel draw near and come to pass, that we may know it!'" The imagery is that of beasts of burden dragging the sins of the people around in decorated floats, flaunting their sins publicly, defying God, and daring Him to judge them—which, in fact,

He did; and which He will do to any nation that defies Him.

This is *the wrath of divine abandonment*: "But My people did not listen to My voice, and Israel did not obey Me. So I gave them over to the stubbornness of their heart, to walk in their own devices" (Ps. 81:11–12). And through Hosea He lamented, "Ephraim is joined to idols; let him alone" (4:17). Sadly, this is the state of the United States of America today.

It has exchanged the truth of God for a lie and has now been delivered over to that lie to become its slave and ultimately be destroyed by it. As a result, God first gave our nation over to *sordid immorality—a violation of His moral order*, then *shameless homosexuality—an inversion of his created order*, and now, a people characterized by *shocking depravity—a disposition of godless corruption*. The psalmist summarized our tragic fate this way: "The wicked will return to Sheol, even all the nations who forget God" (Ps. 9:17). The only hope for any nation or any individual is repentant faith in the Lord Jesus Christ, the subject of the next and final chapter of this book.

3

The Promise of Forgiveness, Deliverance, and Transformation

If anyone is in Christ, he is a new creature; the old things passed away; behold, new things have come.
2 Corinthians 5:17

Scripture is clear, and any honest self-assessment will affirm that we are all sinners. Adam's sin has affected all of us, not only as it relates to the legal guilt that God imputes to us (Rom. 5:18–19), but also with respect to the sinful nature we inherited (Ps. 51:5). Prior to salvation, the disposition of our nature to disobey and displease God was so powerful and pervasive that Paul affirmed, "We were by nature children of wrath, like the rest of mankind" (Eph. 2:3). Nothing about us was pleasing to Him, for "those who are in the flesh cannot please God" (Rom. 8:8). Indeed, "without faith it is impossible to please Him" (Heb. 11:6), because we "were dead in [our] trespasses and sins, in which [we] formerly walked" (Eph. 2:1–2). Wayne Grudem has rightly stated,

> It is not just that some parts of us are sinful and others are pure. Rather, every part of our being is affected by sin—our intellects, our emotions and desires, our goals and motives, and even our physical bodies. Paul says, "I know that nothing good dwells within me, that, in my flesh" (Rom. 7:18), and, "to the corrupt and unbelieving nothing is pure; their very minds and consciences are corrupted" (Titus 1:15). Moreover, Jeremiah tells us that "the heart is deceitful above all things, and desperately corrupt; who can understand it?" (Jer. 17:9). In these passages Scripture is not denying that unbelievers can do good in human society *in some sense*s. But it is denying that they can do any *spiritual*

good or be good *in terms of a relationship with God*. Apart from the work of Christ in our lives, we are like all other unbelievers who are "darkened in their understanding, alienated from the life of God because of the ignorance that is in them, due to their hardness of heart" (Eph. 4:18).[20]

With these reminders of who we were prior to God's saving and transforming grace, every Christian must admit that we bear the same marks of Adam's sin as the most sexually deviant amongst us. Our attitude toward them must therefore never be one of hostility, but one of loving identity. While we are no longer incarcerated in the dungeon of unredeemed humanness, enslaved by sin, we must honestly admit that in varying ways we were once just like them. For this reason, it would be the height of haughtiness to harbor animosity toward even the most sexually deviant. While we abhor their sin, we love them for the sake of the gospel, ever mindful of our own sin and undeserved mercy. After listing a number of life-dominating sins that would certainly apply to each of us in one way or another, Paul made this humbling statement: "*Such were some of you*; but you were washed, but you were sanctified, but you were justified in the name of the Lord Jesus

Christ and in the Spirit of our God" (1 Cor. 6:11; emphasis mine).

Thankfully, God has provided away for sinners to not only be forgiven, but also to be justified, sanctified, and glorified. And this is the ineffably glorious promise of the gospel. Please know there is forgiveness, deliverance, and transformation for those enslaved by illicit sexual desires, including the desires associated with same-sex attraction. Burk and Lambert offer this insightful analysis,

> Sin is not merely what we do. It is also who we are. As so many of our confessions have it, we are sinners by nature and by choice. All of us are born with an orientation toward sin. The ongoing experience of same-sex sexual attraction is but one manifestation of our common experience of indwelling sin—indeed of the mind set on the flesh (Rom. 7:23; 8:7). For that reason, the Bible teaches us to war against both the root and the fruit of sin. In this case, same-sex attraction is the root, and same-sex sexual behavior is the fruit. The Spirit of God aims to transform both (Rom. 8:13). . . . This is not to say that Christians who experience same-sex attraction will necessarily be freed from those desires completely in this life.

Many such Christians report partial or complete changes in their attractions after conversion—sometimes all at once, but more often over a period of months and years. But those cases are not the norm. There are a great many who also report ongoing struggles with same-sex attraction. But that does not lessen the responsibility for them to fight those desires as long as they persist, no matter how natural those desires may feel. The Bible teaches that the Holy Spirit can bring about this kind of transformation in anyone—even if such a progress is not experienced by everyone in precisely the same measure. As the apostle Paul writes, "Thanks be to God that though you were slaves of sin, you became obedient from the heart to that form of teaching to which you were committed" (Rom. 6:7).[21]

The Miracle of Regeneration

God has promised to not only forgive, but radically transform the inner man of those who truly come to Him in repentant faith and trust in Christ as their only hope of salvation. This is the miracle of *regeneration (palingenesia)*, which refers to *a supernatural, instantaneous impartation of spiritual life to the spiri-*

tually dead characterized by both washing and renewal. Paul used the term in Titus 3:5–7: "He saved us, not on the basis of deeds which we have done in righteousness, but according to His mercy, by *the washing of regeneration and renewing by the Holy Spirit*, whom He poured out upon us richly through Jesus Christ our Savior, so that being justified by His grace we would be made heirs according to *the* hope of eternal life" (emphasis mine). This is what Jesus referred to in John 3 when He told Nicodemus, the great teacher of Israel, "You must be born again" (v. 7); "Truly, Truly, I say to you, unless one is born again he cannot see the kingdom of God" (v. 3); and again in verse 5 Jesus said, "Truly, truly, I say to you, unless one is born of water and the Spirit he cannot enter into the kingdom of God."

Regeneration is the Spirit-wrought transformation in the soul that causes an individual to see the dreadful condition of his or her sinful heart and the underserved mercy, grace, and love of Christ that he or she now embraces in saving faith. Every true believer can identify with this—in contrast with the unregenerate that are often "Christian" in name only and therefore remain enslaved to immoral desires.

For example, among homosexuals, same-sex attraction is so strong that they wrongfully assume it is a natural and therefore legitimate expression of their identity which in their mind justifies their same-sex orientation. But as stated in chapter two, whenever the object of one's desire is for that which God forbids, the desire itself is sinful. Paul categorizes it as "the desire of the flesh . . . . For the flesh sets its desire against the Spirit" (Gal. 5:15). And as demonstrated in our previous exposition of Romans 1:24, Paul uses the term "lust" (*epithumia*) to describe evil cravings, immoral desires, and a yearning for that which God forbids. As Jesus stated in Matthew 5:28, "Everyone who looks at a woman with *lust* for her has already committed adultery with her in his heart" (emphasis mine), making lust a manifestation of an immoral heart rooted in our sinful nature. "For out of the heart come evil thoughts, murders, adulteries, fornications, thefts, false witness, slanders. These are the things which defile the man" (Matt. 15:19–20).

So to somehow justify homosexuality on the basis of unbridled same-sex attraction directly contradicts the clear teaching of Scripture where homosexuality is condemned in the same way as "those who are lawless and rebellious . . . the ungodly and sinners . . . the unholy and profane . . . those who kill their fathers or mothers . . . murderers and immoral men and homosexuals and kidnappers and liars and perjurers, and whatever else is contrary to sound teaching, according to the glorious gospel of the blessed God" (1 Tim. 1:9–11).

Truly regenerate people, however, will readily acknowledge that they "formerly lived in the lusts of [their] flesh, indulging the desires of the flesh and of the mind, and were by nature children of wrath," yet the Spirit "made [them] alive together with Christ" (Eph. 2:3, 5). At the moment of our new birth we are made new creatures in Christ, setting into motion a process of sanctification that will culminate in Christlikeness, for "that which is born of the flesh is flesh, and that which is born of the Spirit is spirit" (John 3:6; John 1:13; 1 Peter 1:23). For this reason Paul says, "If anyone is in Christ, he is a new creature; the old things passed away; behold, new things have come" (2 Cor. 5:17).

Solely by the power of God's grace through the agency of His Spirit and His Word, the life of the newborn saint is characterized by overcoming the wicked influences of Satan's world system (1 John 5:4)—and this includes a newfound hatred for what he or she once loved, and a love for what he or she once hated. The Spirit plants within us new desires, loves, passions, inclinations, beliefs, and values so that we are able to "cleanse ourselves from all defilement of flesh and spirit, perfecting holiness in the fear of God" (2 Cor. 7:1).

What a magnificent thing it is to watch the Spirit of God change not only behaviors, but also the very desires of a man or woman's heart—a transformation every believer can affirm, for "we too all formerly lived in the lusts of our flesh, indulging the desires of the flesh and of the mind, and were by nature children of wrath, even as the rest" (Eph. 2:3). And even for the homosexual, I have seen it on many occasions—not that the man begins to have sexual desires for other women in general, for that would be immoral—he will have a godly desire for the wife that God provides for him (Prov. 5:18–19).

Concluding Words of Encouragement and Exhortation

In order for us to glorify God in our body, *we must see our bodies from God's perspective—from a redeemed perspective*. Only then will we be able to honor Him with our body, as we should. We must respect His creation and rejoice knowing that:

1. Our body will be raised up through His power.
2. Our body is a member of Christ.
3. Our body is a temple of the Holy Spirit.
4. Our body has been bought with a price.

We have also learned that when God is ignored and treated with contempt, if they do not repent, He will abandon sinners to the consequences of their iniquities where they will experience a sample of the wrath to come in eternal judgment. Paul describes three stages of this abandonment that can clearly be seen in the collective whole of a culture that magnifies its rebellion against God primarily through its prurience for gross and deviant sexual immorality, each stage being progressively worse in its evil and in its consequences. First, God gives them over to *sordid immorality*, second, *shameless homosexuality*, and finally, *shocking depravity*.

But wherever sin abounds, grace abounds all the more—transforming grace that delivers even the vilest sinner from the slavery of sin and sets into motion a process of sanctification that will one day culminate in Christlikeness.

> For this is the will of God, your sanctification; that is, that you abstain from sexual immorality; that each of you know how to possess his own vessel in sanctification and honor, not in lustful passion, like the Gentiles who do not know God.
> (1 Thess. 4:3–5)

Obviously, no believer can remain passive in this process. We must all "work out [our] salvation with fear and trembling" (Phil. 2:13). We must make it a priority to be "a living and holy sacrifice" (Rom. 12:1) by obeying two crucial imperatives: "Do not be conformed to this world, but be transformed by the renewing of your mind, so that you may prove what the will of God is, that which is good and acceptable and perfect" (Rom. 12:2). For indeed, real and lasting life transformation simply cannot occur apart from a continual renewing of the mind in which the Spirit illuminates the minds of believers so they an understand Scripture when it is heard or read (1 Cor. 2:13–16; Ps. 119:130; Eph. 1:18–19; 1 John 2:27). This process of illumination works in concert with those who labor in serious Bible study (2 Tim. 2:15) and with gifted men who have been called to teach His Word (Eph. 4:11–12; 2 Tim. 4:2) and are devoted to the systematic, in-depth, doctrinal preaching, teaching, and application of the Word that focuses primarily on the character of God and His glorious plan of redemption.

For this reason, Jesus prayed to the Father: "Sanctify them in the truth; Your word is truth" (John 17:17). This requires an intellectual understanding of the propositional truths God has revealed to us in the Bible and a willingness to submit to them in heartfelt obedience. We see this in the apostle Peter's admonition:

> Therefore, prepare your minds for action, keep sober in spirit, fix your hope completely on the grace to be brought to you at the revelation of Jesus Christ. As obedient children, do not be conformed to the former lusts which were yours in your ignorance, but like the Holy One who called you, be holy yourselves also in all your behavior; because it is written, "You shall be holy, for I am holy."
> (1 Peter 1:13–16).

As every mature believer will attest, submission to the Word of God enables us to "walk by the Spirit" so we "will not carry out the desire of the flesh. For the flesh sets its desire against the Spirit, and the Spirit against the flesh; for these are in opposition to one another" (Gal. 5:16–17).

If you struggle with sexual immorality, you must first make sure you have truly confessed and repented of your sin and placed your faith in the Lord Jesus Christ as your only hope of salvation. Many people never find real deliverance because they are not truly born again. But where there is genuine regeneration, the disposition of the soul will be so radically changed that God's desire will become your desires (Ps. 37:15) and He will cause you "to become obedient from the heart to that form of teaching to which your were committed" (Rom. 6:17; *cf.* 1 John 2:23–24). The fruits of genuine repentance and transforming grace will also assure you of your salvation, for indeed, "If you know that He is righteous, you know that everyone also who practices righteousness is born of Him" (1 John 2:29).

While I speak from many years of experience as a pastor, my authority is not of myself but from the Word of God. I've seen hundreds of lives destroyed because they refused to submit to the clear teachings set forth in Scripture, and likewise, I have witnessed hundreds of submissive lives utterly transformed and blessed by God. As a minister of the gospel, I plead with every reader to heed the words of this little book. And as a fellow sinner we can sing "Oh to grace how great a debtor!" and personally affirm the words of the apostle,

> It is a trustworthy statement, deserving full acceptance, that Christ Jesus came into the world to save sinners, among whom I am foremost of all. Yet for this reason I found mercy, so that in me as the foremost, Jesus Christ might demonstrate His perfect patience as an

example for those who would believe in Him for eternal life. Now to the King eternal, immortal, invisible, the only God, be honor and glory forever and ever. Amen.
(1 Tim. 1:15–17)

Endnotes

1   James R. Beck and Bruce Demarest, *The Human Person in Theology and Psychology: A Biblical Anthropology for the Twenty-First Century* (Grand Rapids, MI: Kregel, 2005), 131.

2   https://www.who.int/news-room/fact-sheets/detail/sexually-transmitted-infections-(stis)

3   John MacArthur, *The MacArthur New Testament Commentary: 1 Corinthians*: (Chicago, IL: Moody Press, 1984), 148.

4   John MacArthur and Richard Mayhew: General Editors, *Biblical Doctrine: A Systematic Summary of Bible Truth* (Wheaton IL: Crossway, 2017), 431.

5   Charles Spurgeon sermon, *Believers Free From the Dominion of Sin*, NO. 1410.

6   Thomas Manton, *The Works of Thomas Manton, Volume 21* (Edinburgh: The Banner of Truth Trust, 2020), 29.

7   Thomas Manton, *The Works of Thomas Manton, Volume 5* (Edinburgh: The Banner of Truth Trust, 2020), 223.

8   H. B. Swete, *The Holy Spirit In The New Testament* (London: Macmillan, 1909 and 1921), 181.

9   John MacArthur, *The Gospel According to Jesus: What Is Authentic Faith? Revised and Expanded Anniversary Edition* (Grand Rapids, MI: Zondervan, 2008), 20.

10   Mounce, R. H., *Romans (Vol. 27).* (Nashville: Broadman & Holman Publishers, 1995) 81.

11 https://conqueseries.com/15-mind-blowing-statistics-about-pornography-and-the-church/

12 http://www.familyresearchinst.org/2009/02/medical-consequences-of-what-homosexuals-do/

13 P. H. Davids, *The letters of 2 Peter and Jude* (Grand Rapids, MI: William B. Eerdmans Pub. Co., 2006), 53.

14 Denny Burk and Heath Lambert, *Transforming Homosexuality: What the Bible Says About Sexual Orientation and Change* (Phillipsburg, New Jersey; P&R Publishing, 2015), 72.

15 J. M. Bailey, "Homosexuality and Mental Illness," *Archives of General Psychiatry* 56, no. 10 (October 1999): 883-884.

16 Marshall Houts, *Where Death Delights: The Story of Dr. Milton Helpern and Forensic Medicine* (London: Victor Gollancz Ltd, 1968), 178.

17 http://www.familyresearchinst.org/2009/02/medical-consequences-of-what-homosexuals-do/

18 https://www.healthline.com/health/different-genders

19 https://www.biblestudytools.com/bible-study/topical-studies/what-the-bible-really-says-about-transgenderism.html

20 Wayne Grudem, *Systematic Theology*, (Grand Rapids, MI: Zondervan Publishing House, 1994), 497.

21 Denny Burk and Heath Lambert, *Transforming Homosexuality: What the Bible Says About Sexual Orientation and Change* (Phillipsburg, New Jersey: P&R Publishing, 2015), 58-59.